To you who are ready
to raise hard questions.

Dialogues with Jay

On Life and Afterlife

Donald R. Fletcher

RESOURCE *Publications* • Eugene, Oregon

DIALOGUES WITH JAY
On Life and Afterlife

Resource Publications
An Imprint of Wipf and Stock Publishers
199 W. 8th Ave., Suite 3
Eugene, OR 97401

www.wipfandstock.com

PAPERBACK ISBN: 978-1-5326-1898-7
HARDCOVER ISBN: 978-1-4982-4495-4
EBOOK ISBN: 978-1-4982-4494-7

Manufactured in the U.S.A.

Contents

Acknowledgments

I GLADLY ACKNOWLEDGE MY debt to Plato, in his *Dialogues*, for a pattern of friends meeting to exchange ideas on a major theme. The thoughts here expressed are mine, gathered on life's journey. I claim no authority nor explicit scholarship behind them, but hope that they may serve as a stimulus to talk and reflection. Jay's poem at the end of Dialogue VI is my own.

For help in preparation of the final text I am indebted to my literary consultant, Roger Williams, of Washington, DC, and, supremely, to my daughter Sylvia, who provided encouragement all along the way, with tireless attention to correspondence and to detailed work that would surely have been beyond me.

Donald R. Fletcher

Lions Gate
Voorhees, New Jersey
May 19, 2017

I

I met Lucas in the shade in front of the town hall, as we had agreed. It was his lunch hour, but he said he could extend that. We both knew that Jay—Uncle Jay to many—might want to talk for a while. He'd once asked us to drop the "Uncle," when we were a pair of young graduate students—Luc in chemistry and I in English—setting out to build a log cabin in New Hampshire, and Jay was giving us advice and moral support. Maybe our roles would be reversed now, I thought. Time will do that.

Luc led the way, just two short blocks, to the Athens CCRC (continuing care retirement community). In the lobby, the concierge was brisk, but pleasant. Luc signed us in, and I followed him to Jay's apartment. I wondered how Jay would look. It had been thirty years, and at that time in New Hampshire he was in his prime.

"Jay," Luc was saying, "I told you that Don might be visiting soon. Here he is with me, to see you."

Jay was sitting by an open window, the light directly on a book he was holding. He stood rather quickly, which impressed me, although I noticed that his left hand went to the back of a nearby chair.

His eyes were bright and the hug that he gave me was strong. He was still lean, as I remembered him, and there was a suggestion of the old vigor, even though, expectedly, his face had sagged a bit, leaving deep shadows under his eyes.

"Don, it's so great to see you again! We've both had a lot of years, but I've been with you through some of them. Luc has brought me up-to-date on your travels and accomplishments, your ups and downs."

We stayed a long time that afternoon. Luc assured us that he was free to stay. Jay wanted to talk about us, but in the end we got him to share some of his own reflections.

"Sure," he said. "To get one's existence into focus, I'd say that it helps to be near the end of life, of the here-and-now. But, mortal as we all are, it's a good, healthy thing—not morbid—for each one to come to terms with her or his own death."

He left a pause, so I asked, probing him, "What really is death?"

Jay turned to Luc. "Luc, you're a scientist with a lot of study about the brain. How do *you* define death?"

"Just the brain shutting down," Luc said. "There can be all kinds of causes, of course—disease, drastic injury, injury elsewhere in the body that shuts off the blood flow bringing oxygen, so that the brain cells suffocate. That's what death is, I'd say, in terms of human life."

"What about loss of consciousness or going into a coma?" I asked.

"There the brain hasn't completely shut down," Luc answered. "A part of it is still working, the part that directs involuntary functions like breathing and heart action."

"And if those are sustained by artificial means?" I challenged.

"To somehow keep that much going is not to keep the person humanly alive, in my opinion," Luc said. He turned to Jay. "We know that this isn't a word game—'alive', or 'not alive'. Intense legal battles have been fought over it. The issue becomes the possibility or impossibility of restoring cognitive brain function, which is what defines human life."

"That's interesting," Jay said, joining in. "You suggest that possibly one can keep the body at least partially alive, but that if the cognitive part of the brain has stopped functioning and can't be restarted, that person has died."

"Right," Luc said.

"So," I put in, "when those cognitive brain cells, all the billions of them, are shut down, whether by disease, slow attrition, or by sudden catastrophe, that's the end, the final curtain?"

"That's it," Luc nodded. "Physiologically, that's death."

"Well summarized," Jay said. He left a space for silence in the room. I looked at Luc to see if he might indicate that it was time to leave; but before any move was made Jay was speaking again.

"Well summarized, and for many people—maybe for you, too, Luc—that ends the drama."

"What else?" Luc asked. "For that particular actor, at least, the play has ended. There's nothing more. As Don said, it's the final curtain."

Luc didn't say that dogmatically. He clearly knew that Jay would not agree with him, and I could understand that he cherished Jay's friendship in spite of—or, really, because of—Jay's different point of view.

"You have studied the brain much more than I," Jay was saying to him, "and, I imagine, more than Don, either." I nodded agreement. "You know what is known so far about the functioning of the hundred billion brain cells and the trillions, perhaps, of connections among them—the uncanny mystery of thought and feeling that makes possible the sort of talk and ideas that we've been sharing.

"Now, the marvelous advances of brain science, like any other branch of science, are founded on, and limited to, observation, right? The goal of science, I submit, is the accumulation of information—knowledge—about everything that exists in the universe in which we find ourselves. Such knowledge is objective. It is built up by careful, accurate observation. And the results of such observation, to be reliable, are to be checked, and re-checked—only so, to be added to our knowledge of the universe."

"Yes, I'll buy into that," Luc said. "And according to scientific knowledge, the universe is to be measured and understood along its two dimensions: space and time. Everything we know in the cosmos is conditioned by and belongs to space and time."

"Good," I put in. "I'd agree with that, where knowledge is concerned, and add that in our human curiosity, we've been exploring and pushing out the limits on those dimensions any way that we can. The dimension of space limited our forebears. They could see only as far as the horizon. And when they looked up, they saw sun, moon and stars, but had no real idea of how far away these were. Then human intelligence began to figure out ways of measuring space, of observing and calculating distances."

"And began," Luc said, "to see much further, both out and in, than natural sight could see. More and more instruments were devised, and are being devised, to see deeper and better into outer space, and into the intricacies of inner space as well, the most minute building blocks of matter, of all that exists."

"Agreed," Jay rejoined. "All of these achievements are impressive. We are becoming aware of the vastness of our universe, of an extension of space outward in huge immensity and inward in minute complexity that staggers comprehension. But in all of that I trust that you would agree, Luc, that science builds on what it sees, on what can be observed. What is scientifically factual is what is observed. If it is not observable, it can't be established as fact."

"And the dimension of time," I prompted, curious to see where Jay was going with this. "That appears as another vastness that science has been exploring."

"Exploring in just one direction," Luc added. "Facts can be gathered from the past. The future has to be limited to estimate and hypothesis."

"But it's remarkable—really astounding," I said, warming to a favorite topic, "to consider how much we are learning about our human past—the evidence of human beginnings—for that matter, the evolution on the planet of all forms of life. So much has been uncovered, and can be uncovered, pieced together from scattered fragments that patient searching continues to find."

"All of that on one tiny, more-or-less junior planet," Luc commented, with a shrug of dry humor. "While those paleontologists are digging out and analyzing fossils, a couple of hundred miles above them the Hubble telescope and its successors are peering, and will be peering, into almost unimaginably distant space to observe galaxies so far away and moving away at such speed that the light from them reaching us now is showing them as they were billions of years ago, in the relatively early existence of the universe. That's going far back in time, considering that the current scientific consensus puts the beginning of the cosmos—meaning also the beginning of time—at about 13.8 billion years ago."

"A magnificent perspective!" Jay said. He shifted in his chair and I thought he seemed to be tiring, as he went on. "The achievements of science, all branches of science, are immensely impressive. Our life is greatly bettered by them, and continues to be bettered, even though science is also used for evil and destructive ends that threaten us all—but we'll leave that aside.

"I find still hanging in the air the question with which we began today: what is death? Luc, you gave us, excellently, a scientific answer. Is that all? Is knowledge—the sum of mental acuity—the total, or is there an aspect of human life that we haven't touched on today?"

"I think that there is," I said. "There is soul, spirit, human personhood."

"I thought that something like that would be coming," Luc said. "Don wouldn't let that final curtain close, and stay closed. With enough applause, it might open again."

"And I'm ready with the applause," I told him, "but it's late for bringing that up. We're subject, still, to the dimension of time."

"Right." Luc stood up and so did I. "Jay, we've very much enjoyed being with you."

I added, "It's like old times, only better, after these thirty years."

"Then please come again, both of you," Jay responded, managing again to get to his feet. "Don has ended our one conversation by just beginning another."

We laughed, but we also promised at the door that we'd find another time.

II

FOR OUR NEXT TIME with Jay, Luc brought his daughter Beth, a striking young woman. Some might call Beth beautiful, some not. I'd say that the beauty is in her clear eyes, quickly intense beneath a broad forehead. I was glad that she was wearing her dark hair up, so that it didn't get in the way of her eyes.

"Jay," Luc said, when we were comfortably settled, "I was telling Beth about our conversation, and she said she had to come."

"That is, if you don't have a younger age limit, or an all-male rule," she put in lightly.

"Very glad to have you," Jay said. "Just the perspective that we need."

"Then let me ask about something coming out of the conversation of the other day, as Dad was telling me about it. We're creatures of space and time, part of a constantly flowing stream of life; but each of us would like to think that he or she is unique. If we are, what is that something that makes me, me, and makes you, you?"

Jay turned from Beth to her father. "Luc, does science have an answer for us?"

Luc plainly was ready. "At least a partial answer—partial, as in general our answers need to be, because almost always there's more to be learned. We need to keep pushing out the frontiers of knowledge a bit further. So, about individual personality—what some call personhood—we can consider DNA. We all know that this has been one of the most revolutionizing discoveries of the present era, that we all carry a make-up of genes, complex chemical molecules, that control our physical and mental development. And while there's an overall pattern—a human genome that is what makes each of us a human creature, as distinct from other forms of life—there are also minute genetic variations in DNA that mark each one as a unique individual.

"As we know, analysis of DNA is proving of immense value for criminal investigation and any situation in which a specific human body needs to be identified; but that is secondary. The fact that stands out here is that in our physical make-up each of us is unique, that uniqueness being generated by the genes that we carry. We were born with them, although they can be subject to mutation in ways science is only beginning to understand."

Luc paused. "This sounds like an opening lecture for Genetics 201," he said.

"We're glad to be in your class," Jay responded. "Please go on."

"All right; I'll try to keep it concise," Luc continued. "Genes control the development and function of the brain, along with those of the rest of our physical being. Your brain, in turn—how it functions and what it has been given to function with—is who you are. The brain can be modified. There can be injury, disease, chemical substances, or other factors, and such modification may show itself in apparent changes in personality. There is also the use that you make of the capacities of that brain. Such use is up to you, although it may be influenced—even much influenced—by factors of your heritage and environment. You make choices of the images you store in your brain's memory and the ideas you embrace, pondering them and being shaped by them, as well as competing ideas that you choose to brush aside.

"All of this sets a pattern of function in your brain that is reflected in how you speak and act, and that, as other people see it, becomes part of your personality—part of the person that you are; which means that it is still so: your brain, at any given point in its life development, is who you are."

Luc stopped, then said, with a smile and a shrug, "Well, then, lecture finished. I thought I heard the bell."

"Lecture or not, Dad, that was pretty convincing," Beth said, looking at him with frank admiration.

Then it was Jay, adding, with a cordial smile, "And I'm glad you put it out so well for us. That's why we're here together, I trust—to think, and to speak our ideas as clearly and convincingly as we can. We know we won't always agree, which is healthy, and we know, I'm sure, that no-one will be offended. So, I add my admiration to Beth's: Luc, that was powerfully presented. You know the human brain best of the four of us, and we can't negate what you say about it. My own stance would be just to inquire: having said that, have you said it all?"

He paused, and Beth came in, "Is there more to say, I wonder—anything more that makes each of us the unique person that he or she is?"

I'd been wanting to join in; now I said, "Yes, there is soul, or spirit."

"And what is that?" Beth asked it rather softly. She plainly didn't want to sound combative.

"I'd say it's not a what," I responded. "This is not a thing, as I see it, for which we can give a definition; and that's because it is not part of the space/time cosmos. Our brain, with its marvelously intricate functioning, is. The brain dies off, whether abruptly or by gradual disintegration. As it dies, thinking dies. Emotions flare and fail. Personality may seem to change. Is the essential person dying off, the individual simply ceasing to be? Neurologically, that's the way it appears. What proof is there of anything different? No proof; no fact. Factual, scientific proof requires observation, and here there is no possibility for observation. There can be no tools of space and time capable of reaching outside, beyond, to what transcends space and time. We aren't playing with words here. We're just recognizing that soul, spirit, or whatever word we give it, is that essential being that most of us are aware of, even while, because it is transcendent, no definition and no proof of it is possible."

"That's good," Beth said. "Thank you. It won't convince my skeptical friends, but I say that it's very well put."

Luc twisted in his chair, but Jay was smiling, nodding agreement.

"We're not expecting to convince anyone," he said. "If soul or spirit is real to most of us, so be it. Apparently from far back in the dawning of human consciousness the idea has been there. Now, in these early stages of brain science, we can be pressing to find out where and how the connections may be. Plainly, a good deal may be learned, but I, too, am persuaded that this is not of the stuff of space and time; that it can and does transcend the material cosmos; even though we have no words for describing such transcendence, nor images to picture it. The problem is that our words and images are all just from our present existence."

"Jay," I added, "that thought, that the idea of some sort of soul or spirit seems to go back to the dawning of human consciousness, would appear to be linked from very early with some notion of existence after death. Isn't it so, that from ancient burials and early religious sites on back, humans seem to have believed in an existence after death that wasn't very different from their present life? We find that ancient people, whether in Egypt, China, or the Americas, buried their dead with provisions for a journey or an after-life, even of some grandeur."

"All of which supports the perception," Luc commented, rejoining the discussion, "that the notion of an after-life—including the imagining of it as essentially a continuation of present existence—was and is wishful thinking. Naturally people don't want to die. Those, in particular, for whom life has been good, who have enjoyed rank and prestige, as well as the best comforts their civilization affords, would like to think of this as continuing in some unearthly future realm."

"That sounds cynical," Beth remarked.

"It's not intended to be cynical, just a natural observation," Luc replied. "The hominid branch evolved a species *homo sapiens* with the brain capacity to think, to develop ideas about the life situation in which it found itself. *Homo sapiens* could anticipate and ponder the physical reality of death, and so began to imagine a life beyond death. Very early humanity, long before any kind of records, probably started imagining along such lines, simply to bridge the loss, the finality, of death, and to answer the wish that it might somehow be survived. Something of that comes through, doesn't it, in the early signs of burial and, later, of attempts to preserve or mummify bodies in some way?"

"You keep making a strong case," Jay said. "The question that is left open, I would say, is whether the evidences from human pre-history onward indicate wishful thinking, or a groping after truth. Here we'll agree, I trust, that no objective observation is possible—hence, no scientific fact. There's no doubt about human belief, from very early on, in some kind—or many kinds—of existence beyond death. That's clear enough. But no proof of that existence is possible, because proof, the stuff of science, occurs only on this side of death."

Beth spoke up again, the timbre of her voice a welcome change in the room, I thought. "I'm wondering what it means to speak of this side of death. Presumably this is a human perception of death?"

"Yes," Jay said, speaking rather slowly. "It's seeing death—our death—as a boundary. To cross it is like stepping from one room into another."

"That has to be a long step," Luc put in, with dry humor that had a bit of an edge.

"All right, it is," Jay came back, with patient effort. "It's a major step across, whenever or however each of us comes to that boundary. On this side is our whole present existence, our world of space and time, all that we know. To go across is to transcend it all."

"Which can be scary," I commented feelingly. "Leaving behind everything familiar and known is a frightening thought. From childhood everyone wants to hold onto the familiar."

"Naturally,"—that was Jay, again—"so we naturally fear death; which is sad, since it's the one aspect of life that we all share." Then his voice took on a brighter tone. "But what if death does not mean loss, but gain. Our existence here is bound in, all of it, by the dimensions of space and time, as we've said before. Can we understand that in death we transcend those limiting dimensions? We get beyond them, transcend them. Transcend is the most adequate word I know, even if it's still a space word. The difficulty is that all of our language is language of space and time, as it has to be, time and space being all that we know."

"Isn't that what we are," Luc proposed, with a shrug, "just creatures of space and time?"

"Space/time creatures we certainly are," Jay responded. "But you know I don't accept that we are 'just' that."

Jay began to elaborate, but the essential ideas had already been laid out. After further exchanges that occupied some time, he began to get slowly to his feet and we all stood.

"It's very good of you to come," Jay said, "and I hope you can come again, all three of you. I'd have been happy, in a better time, to have joined you in some more convivial gathering place."

"Background chatter and such conviviality is not what we need," Luc responded. "If you'll have us back, this is a good place to think and share and to let the talk flow."

Beth joined in, taking Jay's hand in both of hers, and we left him, leaning on a chair and waving as we went out the door.

III

IT WAS AN UNUSUALLY warm day for late April when we again arranged to meet with Jay. The Athens CCRC had a patio garden where, at Luc's suggestion, we drew up some wicker chairs on a flagstone pavement in one corner, under leafing trees. Beth brought along a friend, as Luc had taken care to clear with me beforehand.

"Jay," she said, "this is my friend Ian, who specially wanted to meet you and enjoy your conversation."

"Boyfriend?" Jay inquired, with a sly look.

"Well, whatever you want to call him. Boyfriend sounds like a childish term; a special friend, anyway."

Ian was tall, as almost all young men appear to be now, slim and poised. He took the welcoming hand that Jay offered, with due respect, but confidence. I could see that Beth had made a good choice. We settled ourselves, waiting for Jay to take the lead. After just a brief silence, he began.

"Probably we've all been giving more thought to that theme question of soul, or spirit. We agreed that no definition is possible. You effectively expounded, Don, as I recall, how soul or spirit may be a part—even the essential part—of our human make-up; but it is not a thing. It is not to be measured, analyzed, or defined; because, quite simply, it is not of the stuff of our space/time cosmos. Luc would point out that, in that sense, it isn't real."

"Exactly!" Luc took Jay up immediately, as expected. "People can propose all sorts of fanciful ideas; but if these can't be put to a test of objective observation and analysis, they're just ideas, not reality."

I could see that Ian was leaning forward, following each speaker closely.

"Reality," Jay responded. "That's a key word, even a crucial word, here, I'd suggest. For science, so necessary for our well-being and our material progress, the real world is the world of time and space. And there's no question that this is the world we live in, the world we share with all forms of life on planet Earth, and with whatever marvelous, multitudinous forms of existence there may be, scattered among the billions of stars of the billions of galaxies in space.

"All of that is in space. It is observable and knowable within the dimensions of space and time, and they are what define the reality of this universe, this cosmos. I will not argue with that. I entirely accept it."

Jay stopped, but none of us spoke up. We could feel that he wanted and needed to go on. After a few moments, as a light breeze stirred the trees above us, he continued.

"The marvel of humanity, *homo sapiens*, is that the—to me—inscrutable processes of evolution have brought into being a creature so endowed that she—or he—is able to frame in that marvelous brain ideas, abstract concepts, that are not observable nor quantifiable, like the stuff of space and time. They can't be studied, analyzed, in terms of the material cosmos. To most of us, and all through the history we're acquainted with, they are real; but they belong to a reality that is not scientifically knowable. Here are concepts such as compassion, self-sacrifice, even love."

Jay let the words float in the beautiful stillness we were granted, that moment, in that pleasant place.

Beth drew her breath in audibly, and spoke. "I think we aren't alone in that. The animal life that shares our planet shows moving examples of sacrificial self-giving—the parent for its offspring, or one mate for the other."

"True," Luc said. "That's how they have evolved. That's evolution in action, the procreation and enhancement of the species. It's wonderfully interesting to observe; but it doesn't mean that those deer or ants, spiders or any forms of life, are acting out of some lofty moral principle. They're preserving and propagating their species. Natural evolution has selected those with such an instinct, and they instinctively carry out what may appear to some of us as noble, altruistic behavior."

It was Ian, now, who appeared to suck in his breath, but he offered no comment, and Luc went on.

"I remember, from a literature class, our teacher expounding on what is called the 'pathetic fallacy.' It seems that it occurs more often in poetry. The word pathetic is used technically, deriving from the Greek *pathos* and referring to feeling. The fallacy comes in when one ascribes human-like feeling or emotional experience to an object that actually doesn't and couldn't have it. One might speak of a 'pitiless storm,' or of a 'lonely tree' left on a ridge. That's fine for literature, or for a vivid way of speaking, but not for a factual description of natural phenomena."

"All right," I offered, "but what about human feeling? The fact that we use such language demonstrates our emotional response to situations in our lives. However this may have evolved, *homo sapiens* is the only creature we know of who can experience such a range and depth of emotion, and often blend emotion with abstract concepts, such as patriotism, honor, reverence."

Now Ian joined in. It was refreshing to hear a strong young voice, not brash, but thoughtfully assured.

"I would agree with both points of view," he said. "Certainly the pathetic fallacy, common in poetry and in popular speech as well, is just that, a fallacy."

"Ian is a poet," Beth put in, "although he doesn't call himself that."

Ian shrugged, but went on, "Yet, fallacious or not, much of our speech and our thought processes are full of the Greeks' *pathos*, of emotion. Where and when did that come into human development? It seems to be a central part of what defines humanity."

Luc chose to answer Ian's somewhat rhetorical question. "It came in, one may suppose, in the last million years or so. That would be by gradual, almost imperceptible stages, as the advanced hominids were evolving. And it would show that, in some ways, this type of sensitivity helped them to adapt to and cope with their environment. Doesn't it appear that some rudiments of this kind of emotion—crude and simple, perhaps—have evolved in a number of the other more intelligent animal species?"

"Yes, I think they have," Beth supplied.

"Then," Luc went on, "we might question that our emotional responses are something uniquely human that sets us apart. Possibly we're just way out ahead of other species in our evolution."

Jay spoke up: "Luc, we know we can count on you to keep our feet on the ground—even to squeeze a little mud between our toes. The human animal is surely that, a link in the chain of life on this planet. And we are becoming an oppressively dominant link, forcing into extinction far too many other species, even some of the grandest. But still, whenever and however it may have evolved, and whether there are rudimentary traces of it in some other species, we have this human capacity for abstract thought and feeling—for pondering and reflection—yes, even for awe and adoration. And this I join in calling soul or spirit, and I see it as transcendent."

That brought a silence, such that we could hear some distant voices, laughter, and a sound of dishes being gathered up. We weren't totally alone; but after a suitable pause, Ian spoke.

"I would submit that soul or spirit, if transcendent, can only be spoken of in images. Imagination, it seems to me, is one of its main qualities. Sure, this is the brain—a part of the brain—in action. Images, fragments of our space/time experience, are stored up there. Then the imagination, also a mysterious human capacity, brings them out. It perceives or creates relationships among them, making poetic or artistic use of them. It moves those space/time images around, combining and re-combining them, to express fresh and different insights—meanings that it finds in human thought and life—in aspects of our present life, or in aspirations that go beyond it."

Ian stopped and sat looking down, seeming embarrassed that he had spoken so fervently and in such lofty language; but Beth, her face bright, reached over and touched his arm.

This was very much along my line. "Bravo!" I exclaimed. "Well said! And the images that the creative imagination marshals are naturally rich in emotional overtones. What comes in here, I'd say, is another quality of soul or spirit, a sense of beauty. I like the Greek word for it, *ta kalon*, the beautiful, because it also conveyed a sense of the worthy, of what is ennobling. We know, familiarly, that beauty is 'in the eye of the beholder,' and that, whoever the beholder is, she or he belongs to a particular society or culture.

"To say this is just to acknowledge that each of us, as soul or spirit, is very much shaped by and conformed to our environment, our world. Yet we are free to reach outside of it. The artistically creative spirit, in particular, may reach outside by bringing images of that world together in unusual, arresting ways. He or she invites us to explore fresh insights, to think new thoughts and, perhaps, discover an unexpected beauty. These are gifts and capacities of the human soul or spirit."

"Which is to say—not so—that they are gifts and capacities of the human brain?"

That, not surprisingly, was Luc, coming in from his side of the circle. He went on, "Retaining images and shifting them around is a work of memory—and memory is one of the most significant and critical functions of the brain, localized in its specific area. We share memory, of course, with a wide range of life forms on Earth. There is a kind of memory, commonly called instinct, that we only begin to understand. It occurs even in species with only a very rudimentary brain, and it commonly seems to be inherited—that is, transmitted from each generation to the next. It must be part of that species' genetic make-up.

"Here's an example. A little fledgling sea turtle, hatched by the sun's warmth in a burrow on a tropical beach, will wriggle and splash into the sea, and years later—if it's a female and if it's lucky in escaping all predators—now grown to enormous size and weight, it will lumber ashore on that same beach, to dig a burrow and deposit its own clutch of eggs. Over years the swimming turtle has wandered through thousands of miles of ocean, with nothing to guide it. How did it know to find that same beach at that same time of year? We call it instinct. Somehow the turtle's genes remembered and told it what to do—which, Ian, I grant you, is at this point a poetic, rather than a scientific, conclusion."

Jay commented, with obvious pleasure, "Luc, my friend, that was eloquently expressed. I find all evidences of instinct in species other than ours fascinating. They seem to show that memory, some kind of memory, can be claimed for every form of life. The cells of the flower that grows toward the light are responding, presumably, according to the genes in their nuclei. Even those viruses that feed on and destroy our bodies are acting as their genes have evolved to make them act. As for humanity, you know my position, that instinct, which we abundantly possess, has evolved also into our marvelously rich and complex memory, and that our human soul or spirit uses that memory for its thought and creative meditation that seem to be unique."

What more should or could be said about soul or spirit, I wondered. Some large ideas had been set out, to drift around in our garden retreat. We were satisfied to sit in silence for a minute or two.

Then Jay spoke again. "Since you are so kind, all of you, in coming to me for us to share our thoughts, I'll add just one more on that theme of memory. It's natural that in a place like this, where most of us are far down the road of time, memory is important. Memory is conditioned by time—so that it falters as the body and brain falter with the effect of time. Now, we've been talking about soul or spirit, affirming our conviction—some of us— that it's in the nature of soul or spirit to transcend time. That could mean transcending memory. In a transcendent reality, all is present. Such a concept is impossible for us to grasp, conditioned and confined, as we are, in the space/time cosmos; but it can be comforting and reassuring. In a transcendent reality of spirit, memory, the past, is not lost. It is sublimated, as all is present."

Jay paused. "Excuse me," he said. "In talking about that, I have exercised an old man's privilege."

"Exercised it fittingly," I put in. "We're in your debt, Jay; and each time more so, when you welcome us here. Now, we'd better be going along; but I hope there can be another time."

The other three joined in, with expressions of thanks and appreciation; and with that, Jay walked us, a little uncertainly, to the front entrance, and we took our leave.

IV

THE YOUNG PEOPLE ARRANGED for our next dialogue with Jay. Beth said that they wanted to do it. We were into May and they knew of a place at a short drive where there were woods, a small pond, and daffodils. They would have folding chairs in Ian's van, even a small table for wine and cheese. Jay and I could ride comfortably with Luc. They set the day, with a back-up rain date that, in the event, we didn't need.

The day was perfect, the drive only a half-hour, the daffodils in full bloom, and Ian's choice of wine excellent. I had told Luc that by his leave I'd like to turn the talk to ideas about life after death. He'd said, why not? Humanity had always had hopeful notions about that, and anyway we would be talking in a pleasant place, and Beth and Ian could be counted on for good cheese and wine.

Beth sliced and served around a choice of cheeses with crackers, while Ian opened and poured the wine. We of the two older generations settled in our chairs, with Beth and Ian cross-legged on a blanket on the grass. There was some small talk about the beauty and possible history of the place. By now we knew each other well enough to let the talk ebb comfortably into reflective silence. Then, fingering my wineglass, I began.

"I'm thinking of a couplet out of one of A. E. Housman's poems in *A Shropshire Lad*:

> For malt does more than Milton can
>
> To justify God's ways to man.

"Rather than malt, we have some very good wine—thank you, Ian—and a chance, with its help, perhaps, to reflect on our human ways and what may go beyond them. I mean, what may be thought and conjectured about existence beyond death. In the couplet, Housman's whimsical use of the word 'justify' seems to convey a sense of perceiving or understanding justice, that is, helping to see and know the justice of God's ways.

"Now, it appears that very much of what people have thought—and what various religious traditions have taught—about an existence beyond death comes out of ideas of justice. In one of our earlier conversations you argued effectively, Luc, that human notions of life after death have generally tended to reflect a longing that the good things of this present life might continue and might be better and more abundant. You labeled such notions as natural, wishful thinking—people wanting a heaven that is just an idealized version of present life."

"That's right," Luc rejoined, "and in any talk about heaven, I stand by it."

"Good," I said, "but let's press it further. To a large part of humanity it has to appear that life isn't fair. Here are two children born into a family. One is healthy and vigorous; the other shows from infancy a brain defect that leaves her unable to co-ordinate movement, to walk or talk, and subject to frightening seizures and convulsions. Has life been fair to her?"

"How does fairness enter in?" Luc challenged. "It's genetics, the luck of the draw. That's how life works on this planet—how evolution has been coming about from the beginning. It's chance, the chance combination of genes with chance mutation that may result in a stronger or a weaker offspring. There's nothing deliberate about it, no choice, just the chance of nature that is neither fair nor unfair. What humanity can work at learning to do is to off-set the bad outcomes of genetic chance—to control the seizures, to stimulate positive brain develop-ment, even to mend deficiency in specific genes."

"Careful!" Jay broke in, entering the discus-sion. "Science seems to be stepping across the threshold of genetic engineering; although one can say that with selective breeding we've been doing it for a long time. But discussion of that challenging topic as a moral issue could carry us well away from what you had in mind for today, Don. Am I right?"

"Yes, very much so," I responded. "Thanks, Jay. What I wanted to plant is the issue raised by obvious—even glaring—inequalities in our human situation and the effort that is made to cope with them in traditions about an afterlife. Human society isn't capable, on a broad scale, of taking away from the rich and distributing to the poor, to give equally to everyone. Karl Marx popularized the slogan, 'From each according to his ability, to each according to his need,' but Communism has never succeeded in approaching that ideal. So, if we can't achieve an equal distribution of food and possessions in this life, it's natural to hope for it in a life to come."

"And the moral dimension makes it that much more urgent," I went on. "Society may try to punish evil and to reward righteousness, but its efforts are never more than randomly successful. Laws are made, but there are always people who learn to get around them. A perpetual moral issue in this world is the complaint, 'Why do the wicked prosper?' Why are huge fortunes amassed by dubiously legal practices, or simply by callous exploitation of the working poor?

"I think of Browning's verse drama *Pippa Passes*. The naïve working girl Pippa exults in the morning freshness of her one day of freedom in her working year:

> The hill-side's dew-pearled;
>
> The lark's on the wing;
>
> The snail's on the thorn;
>
> God's in his heaven—
>
> All's right with the world.

"Browning's characters go on to demonstrate in his play that all is *not* 'right with the world.' The answer of religious tradition, in many forms, has been that God (by whatever name) is indeed in God's heaven, which is not this world, and that heaven, however it may be conceived, represents an existence beyond death in which the wrongs and inequalities of this life are evened out and all is made just and right."

I stopped. It was my turn to feel somewhat abashed, having gone on so long, but Jay came in warmly:

"Don, I like your reference to Browning's Pippa. Our window today, in this beautiful spot, is open on a world beyond this world, and we'll agree that humanity's religious aspirations have often included a hope that, in such an idealized world or life, earth's wrongs would be righted, and all its evil swept away, by justice, righteousness and peace. Is that wishful thinking? In the here-and-now, the present cosmos, there's no proof and no possibility of proof. The only bridge, for those who see a bridge, is faith."

Now Beth came in, and we were glad to hear a younger voice:

"I'd say that, while it isn't proof, there is, for some of us, a sign or index in present human life. There is a sense of justice. Is it innate, or is it taught to us, learned from society? Maybe it's part of the collective memory passed along from one generation to another. Anyway, that sense of justice urges that the deity—at least in religious traditions that think of a supreme deity in personal form—must be absolutely just. In this world justice may be hard to come by. The wicked prosper. Human evil gets the upper hand. But there is a sense of justice, that our existence has a boundary of moral law, not just of chance, to be exploited selfishly in any way possible. And that sense of justice supports, also, a sense that this life isn't the whole story."

I was impressed. The young people were fully on a par with any of us, on a level of thought and reflection.

"Right," Ian said, leaning forward in his perch on the blanket. "I wouldn't at all want to launch into a discussion of comparative religion. Enough, I think, just to take note that in most religious traditions that include some kind of survival of the person beyond death, in whatever form, there is a summoning to judgment, an arraignment before the godhead. No escape is possible, nor any false pretense."

"Quite true," Luc said, entering the discussion. "Please don't think, the rest of you, that I like to take an adversarial position. I respect religious faith and acknowledge gladly the huge contributions that various religions, in their better aspect, have made toward gentling and even ennobling human society. It's on the other side, as I see it, that organized religion has exploited the idea of a divine judgment. That idea has been used to intimidate people—even, at an extreme, to terrorize them—into submissive obedience to what the religious authorities desire. 'Do this, accept this, conform to this, or God will cast you into eternal hellfire.' The intimidation can take many forms, crass or subtle. It can be a threat of torment in another world, or simply of a debased reincarnation in the present one. Religion uses the afterlife as organized society uses the present life, to secure a desired behavior by offering a prospect of reward on one hand and punishment on the other."

Jay responded to that. "Luc, no-one can deny, especially now, the point that you make. We are witnessing in this early twenty-first century something of the savagery and brutality that religious extremism can inspire. We mustn't shut our eyes to that. It is being used, as in other forms and other times it has been used, to justify terrorism and appalling oppression.

"Let's leave it at that today. Ian and Beth, might we have another round, along with a little of those delicious cheeses? I'd like to raise a glass to the good in human hearts everywhere, to what is generous and noble and God-inspired, while each one thinks of God as she or he is glad to do."

The wine went around, and we raised our glasses, touching them together, as I would say that our spirits touched, pledging glad thankfulness to life, life of the Spirit, among us then and there, as here and now.

After that happy interlude, and when it was quiet enough for us to hear a soft lapping of ripples as a breeze across the pond was sending them ashore, Jay spoke again:

"You know, all of you, I think, that three years ago Rachel left me, or was taken from me. My dear friend Luc, you were right there with me. It wasn't that she died that evening. The certificate said so, with date and time; but as the relentless shadow of Alzheimer's gradually eclipsed her brightness, you could say she had been dying across our last fifteen years together. Enough of that; I bring it in because we are talking about an existence beyond death— an existence that, as my faith would affirm, ties in with what I've known and cherished, but is much more. My mind wants to ask, where and how? Mind, this present mind, stops at the boundary. We recognize—and Luc put it clearly in our first talk together, before you joined us, Beth and Ian—that the brain shuts down. The reality that we know, the here-and-now of this existence, ends for that person, that loved being. The dear, familiar warmth of breath and pulse stops. Whatever is done with the body—become suddenly useless and even alien— we need to do soon, within only hours; which is all right, because that is no longer the loved person. She isn't there."

Jay paused. I was shaken; I think we all were. Could he go on? After a moment, he did.

"Now, what I say—what anyone says—is said in a language of faith. There are no clear terms. There is no knowledge, no possibility of proof. We've been through that. I myself stand historically in the religious tradition of Christianity, in the Reformed branch of Protestant faith. It's true that Christians, as also Jews and Muslims, hold generally to some idea of a resurrection after death. That would mean, presumably, to a restoration of that person recognizably to the individuality by which he or she was known in earthly life.

"For Christians, the ground of such a belief is the resurrection of Jesus. The Apostle Paul, first-generation Christian leader whom I admire, was very strong on this. In fact, his faith and his teaching were built on a mystical conviction that he was frequently, if not constantly, in personal communion with the risen Jesus. In the great fifteenth chapter of the writing that the Church knows as his First Letter to the Corinthians, Paul declares the foundational reality of Jesus' resurrection, as a promise of the resurrection of all believers.

"There he responds to the natural question as to what sort of body this resurrected body may be. His analogy is the seed planted in earth, which sprouts into a quite different form. So, he says, what is planted in earth as a physical body is raised a spiritual body. That is as much as he can say.

Certainly for Paul that resurrection of Jesus Christ was reality. Without it, he declares, his whole gospel message is false, a delusion.

"One has to respect Paul's fervor, and I embrace it. But if he could come down that path through the woods and join us here, I'd try to explain, over the glass of wine I'm sure he would accept, how the reality we are affirming in faith is not fact for us, because it is not subject to factual proof, as our present life is. Paul's 'spiritual body,' his resurrection, is not real as a part of this reality. But I'd declare it, as I believe Paul would, as transcendent reality—a reality of God's transcendence. That's enough; that's where my love is invested."

Jay said that last line softly, almost meditatively, looking across the water. Then he turned, abruptly and purposively bright:

"But here we are, together in this lovely spot. Let's relax a little and enjoy it."

"I'm for that," Luc said.

He stood, and went quickly down to the pond's edge, bending to pick up a stone that he had evidently been eyeing. It was smooth and flat. With a quick swing, he sent it skipping across the water, all the way up to lodge in a soft bank on the far side. Beth took up the challenge, and Ian, hunting for stones of the right size and shape and sending them flying across, with laughter that splashed like the stones making rings of ripples on the water. I tried my hand, too, going back to boyhood and a smooth stream that was far away.

When we came back from that to Jay and our circle, we needed the jug of water that Beth had kept cool in the picnic chest under a thick bush. We were all familiar friends now, to joke and kid one another, and Jay was enjoying it.

"Next time," he said, "I'll bring some horse-shoes and a stake, for you to try. That level area down by the water would do fine; but they need to be real horseshoes, like they put on the Budweiser Clydesdales."

"All right," Luc came in, "you're on! And I'll bring the beer, but maybe not Bud. I like some of these 'craft' brews that our locals are producing."

There was more talk and laughter, and then a pause. I think the other four of us sensed that Jay had something he wanted to add in a more serious vein. We sat again in our circle and Jay began.

"A last thought or two on our theme of today: existence, being, beyond this world and life. Am I simply indulging in imaginative conjecture? Per-haps so. Come along with me, if you will, while we give it a try. What seems clear is that the bound-ary of this life, for each of us, is the boundary of space/time experience. These are the dimensions that limit us. If there is for us any kind of personal existence beyond them, it means freedom from them—freedom from space, the tangible, material substance of a body that we inhabit, with all of its constraints; freedom from time, the inexorable aging and decline of that body, hastened by disease, affected by whatever accidents occur. How would it be for the soul or spirit to be liberated from any and all of those constraints? We are identified by our bodies, the physical part of us. The genes, the DNA, that mark each individual as the unique physical organism that goes by her or his name—that's who we are.

"Or so it seems to be, until one steps over the boundary. Then my spirit affirms that her spirit is still there—not there spatially, temporally—not to be touched or held, not to be seen, but existing, real, in a reality that transcends what I am able to know. And although I can't now touch or feel or see her, there is a contact I can make, a spiritual sense, for which the word most used is love. Spirit can reach through to spirit. This is all figurative language; we don't have any other. The reality that is beyond is unknowable to us, here and now. Only spirit can affirm it by that power of spirit, which is love."

Jay went silent. My heart surged to see his face. Perhaps it was just the late sunlight rippling off the water, that it seemed there was a glow for that moment.

Then Jay said, "Enough. Thank you for indulging me; now it's time to be gathering up, thinking about our homes and dinner and good things we still have in our universe of space and time."

V

I was meeting Luc at some time every weekend in those days. You must understand that I was single, a freelance writer, and that my recent novel was doing very well, well enough to allow me freedom to settle for a time not far from Luc's address. On this Saturday, when we got together he took me to the marina, saying he wanted me to see his boat. She was beautiful, secured there in her slip, her tall mast swaying just a little from the controlled wakes of launches passing up or downstream in the main channel.

"I thought," Luc was saying, "that we could get together with Jay next Sunday afternoon here on the boat. The marina has a small gangplank and we could help him on carefully."

Of course I was delighted with the idea. So, when the time came, the five of us, in high spirits, were making our way along the marina's piers to Luc's slip, then helping Jay and jumping after him, to comfortable seats on boat cushions in the aft cockpit of Luc's sloop. The afternoon was perfect, with a light but steady breeze fluttering a pennant at the masthead.

On Jay's urging, Luc started the inboard motor, Beth and Ian cast off the mooring lines, and Luc eased the sloop out to the main channel, then past the breakwater toward the open bay. There he turned her bow into the breeze and we ran up the mainsail and unfurled the Genoa jib. That was a beautiful thing to feel and see, the sails filling and taking graceful form, as the sloop heeled over just moderately and a chop began lapping at the bow. Astern a wake was forming, with the beacon on the breakwater soon shrinking down.

We sailed for an hour and more—I didn't keep track of the time, nor of where we were. Then Luc brought us under the lee of a small island and had us anchor there, dropping and furling the sails. He went into the cabin, to bring out a folding table, a picnic chest, and other items. Beth, as hostess, helped deftly to set out a tempting supper. The sheltered water where we were was so calm the sloop hardly moved under us as we sat around the horseshoe of the cockpit's cushioned seats, enjoying the meal. At the end Ian brought fragrant, steaming coffee from the galley, to supplement the wine Beth had been pouring. Then she and Ian cleared things away, folded and stowed the table, and we sat with just our coffee or wine, in reflective mood in the warm, late-afternoon light.

After a little, Jay began: "Out of the depths of childhood memory come words of a hymn for a setting and time like this." He started to sing uncertainly, but Beth caught up the tune in a firm, flowing voice. She plainly had been conversant with the church, in one of its traditions, as she was growing up.

> Day is dying in the west;
>
> heaven is touching earth with rest.
>
> Wait and worship, while the night
>
> sets her evening lamps alight
>
> through all the sky.
>
> Holy, holy, holy,
>
> Lord God of hosts,
>
> heaven and earth are full of thee;
>
> heaven and earth are praising thee,
>
> O Lord Most High!

We had all joined in; it seemed that each one had been touched by that hymn somewhere along the line.

When it was finished, Jay went on: "'O Lord Most High.' Humanity has used so many names—conjured up so many pictures—for that overarching aspiration. The discussion I'd like for us to share today, on this evening, is in the sphere of faith. Luc, I mentioned evening, and it's true that the day is wearing away. You need to tell us how long we can talk, because you're our captain and we don't want to be at sea in the dark."

"Don't worry," Luc answered. "The air is clear. If we're still here at dusk the shore lights will be coming on. The breeze will die, but we have plenty of fuel and I've slipped in past that breakwater many times after dark."

"Good," Jay said, "then we can go on. This seems an ideal setting and time of day for pondering the thoughts we may have of God. Not God's thoughts. Now, at the very beginning, we will remember the prophet's admonition:

> For my thoughts are not your thoughts,
> nor are your ways my ways, says the LORD.
> For as the heavens are higher than the earth,
> so are my ways higher than your ways
> and my thoughts than your thoughts.

(Isaiah 55:8, 9 NRSV)

"And we will also acknowledge one more time that we have no language for transcendence. We can only use pictures—inadequate pictures, that we take from our own life-experience."

He paused, and so Luc came in, but in a peaceable tone, "So, what more can be said? Is there any use trying?"

"We can well ask," Jay responded. "If we try to say anything definitive, comprehensive, about the being of God, we would do better to close our lips and be silent. Our best thoughts fall far short. In fact, the descriptive words we usually use are simply negatives—words like immortal, invisible, incomprehensible, unknowable. But in our human sphere, from humanity's earliest inklings represented in signs or symbols, we see awareness of some kind of spiritual presence, and a groping after names for God. And we ask, is this all just from our side of the boundary? Is it just a natural, spontaneous, human thing?

"No doubt, to a considerable degree it is. As humans became aware of themselves as persons, they would also tend to personify the forces of nature with which they had to contend. They would think of the storm, the cataract, the sun and moon, as personal beings. And because they needed and wanted to have some control over these forces, and not simply to cope and survive as other animals did, they addressed the personified forces as spiritual beings, gods and goddesses, with superior powers. Such beings should be worshiped, and perhaps, through worship, be persuaded to help and benefit the human worshiper.

"Isn't it true, that this kind of reasoning and motivation, developed and elaborated in more sophisticated ways, appears to underlie humanity's many religious traditions? Distinctly included in such an analysis is the natural force of death—of aging and mortality—and a longing to be able somehow to go on living, even living more fully and happily than the natural world allows?"

Jay paused, and I expected Luc to say something, but he may have felt that he didn't need to. Jay was saying it for him. Then Jay went on.

"Many elements of humanity's religious traditions are traceable to this kind of motivation. The forces or the issues of life are too great for an individual or a social group to cope with them. But if one can approach a spiritual being, a divinity, that is behind them and secure that divine being's favor, then all will be well; then rain will fall, enough and not too much; then children will be born and will grow up; then war will be avoided, or one's own side will be victorious.

"The divine beings are thought of in very human terms, to be flattered and won over by gifts and offerings, by faithful observance of ritual, even by extreme forms of sacrifice. So religious tradition develops. A priestly caste emerges, charged with maintaining the tradition—its mystique and power. An increasingly elaborate and influential structure of organized religion takes form. All of this appears as humanity's quite natural creation, born of natural human need."

Jay stopped, and there was silence. Where was he going with this? Puzzled, I tried to see how the others were reacting, without seeming too curious. A few ripples moved the boat under us just slightly, and then Beth spoke:

"Jay, I think we all have to acknowledge the validity of what you've outlined regarding organized religion, whatever the particular tradition. So, what comes next?"

Jay answered, "Next, I think, is to ask about the other side, about what is beyond the boundary of our present human existence. Certainly most organized religions have their traditions about that. Their founders or special figures are held to have received, or to continue to receive, communications from the divine. Such communications may be preserved as sacred writings, scriptures. And there are those who claim to have, or to have had, epiphanies, direct insights. All of this has to do with the other side. Its effects are in this space/time world, but its claims go beyond, and therefore there is no proof. Luc, you would agree?"

"Exactly so," Luc said.

"Well then," Jay went on, "we are on a terrain of faith. We've spent a few minutes reminding ourselves with candor of all the very human motives and motifs mixed in with humanity's religious ideas. There are elements that have produced both noble and hideous actions. But approaching as close as we can to our space/time boundary, we ponder about the other side, about what may be beyond it. The soul or spirit within us—as we've talked about it—affirms a reality—reality that is transcendent, as compared to our here-and-now. Our spirit affirms the Spirit, transcendent Spirit, God. Our small being, our fleeting existence, the entire frame of our universe of time and space, is held in the purpose and will of God. Faith catches a glimpse of that—is staggered as it tries to comprehend."

The sound of Jay's voice stopped. Instinctively I looked up, as I believe some of the others did. The sun had set, dropping down behind the island. Our masthead, a dark shape, appeared to ride among pink-tinted clouds.

It was Ian who ventured a comment. "The Spirit, God, moves our small spirit. God shakes us, I believe, and has inspired the best and highest that humanity has achieved."

"Yes, Ian," Jay responded, "and how good to hear it from your generation, more than from mine. And so, we need to restore a balance to what we said about humanity's religions. As the Spirit, God, is Source of all and cares for all, surely humanity is not left simply to grope from our side. We won't pretend to know what are the ways of God, but we may declare our faith that, as our spirit tries in fumbling ways to reach for the Spirit, the Spirit reaches through to us. We won't attempt, certainly not here this evening, to consider each epiphany or alleged epiphany; but surely it must be so, that God, whose love we will affirm to be impartially for all, has been granting insights, making known something of God's self, to many people in many times and places.

"Sadly, there is a tendency among religious traditions to claim unique and authoritative truth, God's special revelation given only to and through that tradition. Can such teaching concur with a faith in God who loves and cares for all? In God's providence, we are born, each one of us, into a particular religious tradition, that of a particular culture at a particular stage of its development. Let's acknowledge this with appreciation and trust; but, also, recognize that no particular tradition, no religious teaching, can comprehend the whole truth of God."

As Jay paused, now it was Beth who came in: "I'm glad to hear you put it that way. In human history each culture, as it seems, has its saints and visionaries, its men and women who are honored and remembered for their insights. Followers gather around them. What they have written, or has been written about them, comes to be a part of scripture that is sacred to their adherents. Has God truly spoken through them? How can we know?"

"I'd say we can't know," Ian rejoined, "not in any final way; but as a test, we can consider the result. What has a particular religious tradition produced? Is the world better for it, or worse? That sounds simplistic, and human life is not simple; but I think there are broad effects that can be traced."

Now Luc spoke up: "There I would agree. Talk about so-called 'spiritual things' leaves me unconvinced. And as for religion, we see, and have seen, too much violence and oppression perpetrated in the name of God and the gods. What does religion do for people? How does it advance humanity, the human condition? That is something realistically measurable."

"True," Jay responded, again taking hold of the discussion, "and in this exchange I am expressing a conviction that transcendent God cares for all people, from when they weren't yet people, and that, as God's way of creating humanity has seemed so astoundingly gradual and prolix, so what God reveals of God's Self seems to be given in brief glimpses, spread across a broad range of cultures and of time, and imperfectly understood. Our side is to ponder these glimpses with thoughtful respect, quite conscious that when any human speaks of God, she or he is speaking of transcendent Being."

Jay let that linger. Dusk was coming on now, and our faces around the circle were less distinct. After a few moments I offered a comment.

"We won't pretend to think God's thoughts, nor to describe God's ways. Surely God is unknowable, unimaginable—according to all images that we can conjure up, which are only of space/time. Out of our provisional being we affirm by faith that God is absolute Being. But is God totally different, and therefore inaccessible to us? One stream of theological thought accentuates the difference, even to an extreme of asserting that God is the *Totaliter Aliter*, the Wholly Other. That, I would say, would be an appalling conclusion. It would shut away from the human spirit any possibility of communion with the Divine."

I paused a moment, then went on. "The three Abrahamic faiths hold, rather, to a belief in the divine Personhood. God is perceived as revealing God's self as Self, that is, as the Person, supreme and absolute. And humanity, as in the creation narrative in Genesis, chapter 1, is seen as being made 'in the image of God.' The picture does not at all suggest that we are human gods and goddesses, but that, with all our human foibles and propensity toward evil, there is yet in us a capacity of spirit to reflect, however dimly, the Spirit, and to commune in our humanly limited way with God, our Maker.

"It appears to be God's choice, I would suggest, to grant to particular men and women at particular places in human history some compelling visions of God's truth; which visions need to be sifted and pondered carefully, as we've said. They may be surprising, even revolutionizing, in their effect on society; but if they are truly of God's revealing, they will prove to be in harmony with God's Spirit, who, however dimly, is within us."

Jay stirred and responded, "Don, I think that is well said, and is as much as any of us can say, on this side of the boundary. Perhaps we need to leave it there for now, and ask our Captain Luc to take command, to get his vessel—and us—back safely to its slip, as he knows how to do."

With that, we all stirred. Beth climbed to the foredeck to take up the anchor, while Luc started the motor. Soon we were out of the island's lee; there were lights twinkling along the shore; and, as I looked up, the masthead light was on, showing bright against a dark sky.

VI

I WAS STARTLED. JAY had invited the other four of us to meet him in his apartment at 2:00 on a Sunday, several weeks after our evening on the water. When we arrived, a woman in a white coat met us at the door. Jay was just beyond, but seated, wearing cotton pants, an open-neck shirt, and with bare feet thrust into slippers.

"Come on in," he called; then, as we entered, "This is Lois, one of our excellent nurses; and, Lois, these are my friends Luc, Don, Beth and Ian," indicating each one. To us he said, "Please forgive my appearance and my staying seated. Such are my orders; but I'm so glad you've come."

We began to protest, of course, that it was fine, but that we'd come back at a better time.

"No," he said, "this is a good time and we're all here. Lois was just checking my vital signs—you know what that's like."

In a pleasant manner she assured us that all was well with our being there and that she needed to be on her way. So, we seated ourselves a bit hesitantly. Jay took a sip of water, smiled around our group, and began.

"I'd like to take up, in some measure, where we left off a couple of weeks ago in that idyllic setting. My living room has nothing to offer like your boat, Luc; but the theme is grand enough and our group is the same. We were pondering the broad compassion of God, as we believe it to be, which makes known something of God's self through glimpses, brief epiphanies, across human history. We can't say comprehensively where these are given, nor how often.

"We believe there is a movement of the Spirit reaching human spirits in many places and many ways. Our spirit is often sluggish and unresponsive. How many insights, revelations, has God offered, and they have been ignored or, worse, have been distorted, misinterpreted, declaring a message that surely God did not intend!

"'Now there you go,' someone objects, 'presuming to say what God intends, or does not intend!' That's right; we must be cautious and reticent in any assertions about epiphanies granted by transcendent God. But we need to ponder and evaluate. As we survey the scene of religious insights, present and past, of revelations and epiphanies that people claim to have, or to have had, we need to assess all such claims as far as we are able. God knows us intimately, all of us, and cares. This we believe. So, it follows that God has been revealing God's truth where and how God chooses, according to human capacity to receive and comprehend it.

"There can be no monopolies here. No single visionary, nor group of adherents of that visionary, can claim possession of the whole truth of God. Actually, given our natural human limitation, plus the further limitations of historical bias and social prejudice, it may seem surprising that God is able to get through to us at all."

As Jay paused, Ian spoke up.

"Jay, I have to share your discouraging, not to say pessimistic, assessment of the religious scene. Our quest for spiritual truth seems, much of the time, to be more a battle than a quest. Instead of listening to one another, acknowledging by faith that all are given life by one Creator and seek the inspiration of one Spirit, religious traditions fight and tear each other down. The fiercer they hold to their own insights—what they insist are truths— the more fanatical they become, strewing the pages of history with crusades, pogroms, beheadings, even genocides. Those who are moderate make enlightened efforts toward interfaith dialogue and cooperation, but theirs is a lonely enterprise."

"Ian," Jay said, "you've summed up the reality. It's sad—in fact, it's tragic—that strongly held religious conviction veers so easily into fanaticism, and any balance of an open mind or spirit is lost. But let's shift our focus away from these too-human flaws, away from the negative to the positive, away from hate to love. In the Christian scripture of the New Testament, it is the mystic, in the writing commonly called the First Letter of John, who urges,

> Beloved, let us love one another, because love is from God; everyone who loves is born of God and knows God. Whoever does not love does not know God, for God is love.

(John 4:7, 8 NRSV)

"This is a sweeping, radical teaching. There are no nuances of doctrinal statement. God, as affirmed here, is the one God of Abrahamic faith, sole and absolute, the Transcendent, and to love, this mystic declares, is to be born of God and to know God.

"To be sure, our mind quickly feels a need for qualifying considerations, but the mystic offers none. He (or she) is proclaiming absolute Love, Love that is God's Self, transcendent and beyond. But he is also affirming on our human level that whoever loves is born of God and knows God. How is it possible to have so intimate an experience of the ineffably Divine? That would have to be reserved for some few rare and privileged souls, some spirits dedicated to an intensely devotional life. No, the mystic declares it for 'everyone who loves.' Well then, this loving must be something far beyond what we ordinary people think of as love. No, the writer is generally addressing the people of his community of faith, calling them 'beloved' and urging that all should 'love one another.'

"We look out on our world. We see where there is love—simple, unheralded glimpses of it between parent and child, between spouses in the sameness of a long-term marriage, between the leader and the follower when they acknowledge their need for one another; romantic love as well, when there is genuine regard of each for the other. Love, wherever you find it in all the tortuous maze of human relationships—that is of God.

"The vision is seldom seen in awesome splendor. It is more likely to be glimpsed, I think, in common garb, in ordinary, everyday moments when the heart reaches out, in the kind, spontaneous gesture, the self-giving with no expectation of return. These are of God. No-one may seem to notice, but God is there. We thank God for the exalted epiphanies, the rare and privileged visions of prophets and sages that are given for all of us to ponder; but the greater treasure of God's self-revealing, as I believe, is in a simple, daily experience of compassion. It is in ordinary life made extraordinary by a frequent inner communion with the Spirit, who is Love, a communion which prompts also a reaching out in compassionate love to those around us—to those we naturally love and those naturally unloved. Transcendent Love is surely able to include them all—every one."

Jay stopped, leaning back in his rocking chair. I thought he looked tired, and we all let a few moments pass, becoming aware of movement in the hallway usual to a community like his.

Then Luc spoke. "Jay, you make the case well for a supreme Being who is Love. I'll heartily agree that such religious teaching as that can help us all in our living together on this planet. Also, I'm mindful of the caveat expressed in our previous time together, that our thoughts and ways are not God's thoughts and ways. A transcendent Being is not to be fitted into any system of human logic.

"That said, I find a problem in matching the natural order of life on Earth and a creating God who is love. The driving principle of life here is survival, which includes competition for the means of survival, which are always limited. Add to that the basic factor of evolution, which appears to be built into the order of life by the Creator—if one posits that there is a creative purpose in our universe, and not just chance. Evolution, operating gradually over long periods of time, means a proliferation of species of all sorts. This is marvelous, even beautiful to contemplate, as I would readily agree; but for the thought of God as Love there is a problem.

"Species, competing to survive on a planet of limited resources, evolve capacities to prey on one another. It comes to be that life survives by consuming life. In fact, we humans evolve to be the supreme predators. We sustain our life by eating many other forms of life, and those we don't literally feed on, we squeeze hard by taking over for ourselves the natural resources that they depend on for survival. Behind it all is the simple reality that life on this planet exists by competing to survive, a competition up and down the chain of being that includes one species inflicting pain, suffering and death on another."

"That's very strong, Luc," I said, "but you're putting it as it is. This is no Pollyanna sort of creation. Witness an outbreak of Ebola in Liberia. Where did the virus come from? How did it evolve? Faith affirms that there is only one Creator. If the all-comprehending principle is love, then Love wills also this suffering and death."

"Yes," Beth broke in quickly, "but love's also present in the response, in those doctors and nurses risking their lives to try to halt the epidemic, and in all compassionate effort to block the progress of disease and to improve the quality of life."

Now Ian joined in. "Sure, we find it easy to discern God's love in altruistic actions that use the best of human intelligence to ease pain and to heal body and spirit; but the problem Luc posed is still here. For the forms of life on our planet, including humanity, presently at the top, conflict, suffering and death are built in from the beginning. One line of religious thought, as I've run across it here and there, declares belief in a duality, a god or force of evil, perpetually in conflict with a force for good.

"The monotheism of the Abrahamic faiths won't accept that. The one God, just and righteous, is sole Creator and Controller of all. No wonder that an off-shoot has been the idea, variously developed, of a Satanic power, a spirit of evil to whom God allows limited power temporally, before a final judgment. I don't find anything satisfactory in that. To me, the problem of a loving Creator and a creation abounding in what can be called natural evil has to have a higher solution."

"Do you have one?" Luc asked.

"No and yes," Ian answered. "That sounds like a typically philosophical evasion, which it isn't meant to be. I can't have a solution, because I can't know the thoughts and ways of God, but I believe we can affirm by faith that because God is God, God's transcendent Love can embrace all sides of the problem. Our experience of love is limited by our human nature in our space/time cosmos. We can affirm by faith that transcendent Love is with us, sharing, beyond our comprehension, every struggle, every grief and pain, every agony of spirit, assuring us that all has purpose and can mean a blessedness beyond the boundary of our here-and-now."

Ian's voice had risen a little, intensity radiating from him, lapping us all in a pool of silence. Jay had sat with head bowed. Now he looked up and spoke.

"Love—transcendent Love—that's where our ultimate focus needs to turn and hold. We have our inklings, our dim experiences of love, and they are the richest, God-endowed pieces of our humanity. Faith glimpses, above and beyond them, transcendent Love, complete and absolute. Faith exults, in joyful adoration. This is God, transcendent, while also wonderfully near and intimate. Again, we have only glimpses, and we grope for images to try to say what the spirit within us is sensing.

"Now, I'd like to return today to where our conversations began a good many weeks ago, that first time, Don, when Luc brought you and we talked together about the end of life, reaching the boundary. An image I have found helpful to express that edge and boundary is of a beach and the eternal sea. When Rachel slipped away from me three years ago, it was late November. Some five weeks later, on New Year's Day, the lines of a lyric poem came to me, to gather up what I was experiencing. May I share it with you?"

Jay paused, and there were nods, expectant looks, but no spoken response, so he went on, giving us the poem.

> The beach is there as in moonlight, more felt
>   than seen,
> and your hand yet in mine, or not, I still can feel,
> warm and serene, the shaking gone. My love,
> you slipped away in the moonlit deep, your breath
> a gentle wisp, and this eternal sea,
> full and strong, lifting and carrying you.
>
> I am content—alone now on the beach,
> but with the far shore nearer, and your love

free now and with Love blending. Let it be,
and let those prints you left down to the gentle
surge, withdraw and surge be on my heart
printed in promise: we will walk again,
hand in hand, will run and frolic on
the unimagined shore, where God is all,
and all is God, beyond the eternal sea.

"That was how Rachel went, at the end of the long, relentlessly declining arc of Alzheimer's. The image of the moonlit deep is not meant to be frightening. And of course, with the unimagined shore I've taken the sort of liberty that I've cautioned against taking—imagining an existence that repeats happy moments of this life—walking hand-in-hand, even running and frolicking, as she hadn't been able to do for years, with her illness. Well, we can have our images—mine of the beach and the footprints down to the lapping water. God's love understands and embraces us all."

Jay stopped, and I was aware that Lois, the nurse, had opened the door quietly and been standing just inside.

"Jay, that is beautiful," I said, "too beautiful for any more words. We can take it with us now, as we go along."

One by one we hugged him, not trusting ourselves to speak, then said smiling, low-voiced words to Lois at the door, as we left.

Epilogue

THREE DAYS LATER, IN the afternoon, we each received the word from Athens CCRC, learning afterward that Lois had insisted that we should be called, each one.

In the evening we gathered at Luc's home. He had brought out a very special bottle of wine, and when the time was right and he had poured our glasses, I proposed a toast:

"To Jay, for his wisdom and his love, for what he taught and how he was, and is."

We drank the toast, and then Beth raised her glass again:

"For Jay and Rachel, who and how they are, on the unimagined shore."

Luc added, "And their God, who is All."

Other works by
Donald R. Fletcher

I, Lucas, Wrote the Book
Xlibris, 2003

    (an imaginative recreation of the writing of the Third Gospel)

View From the Playroom Floor
Xlibris, 2004

    (contemporary philosophical/theological reflections)

Turnings: Lyric Poems Along a Road
Outskirts Press, 2009

    (a combined memoir and anthology of personal poems)

The Gift: Looking to Jesus As He Was
CreateSpace, 2010

    (an analytical study of historical traces of Jesus in the Gospels)

Martha and I: Life, Love and Loss in Alzheimer's Shadow
Wipf and Stock Publishers, 2017 (republished)

    (an account of the long struggle with the author's wife's illness, combined with scenes of her as she was throughout her earlier life)

By Scalpel and Cross: A Missionary Doctor in Old Korea
Resource Publications, Wipf and Stock Publishers, 2016

    (the story of a Presbyterian medical missionary told against the background of Korea in the first half of the twentieth century)